T0300672

Say It With Me

I was looking for trouble to tangle my line
But trouble came looking for me

— RICHARD THOMPSON

Say It With Me

Vanessa Lampert

Seren is the book imprint of
Poetry Wales Press Ltd.
Suite 6, 4 Derwen Road, Bridgend, Wales, CF31 1LH
www.serenbooks.com
facebook.com/SerenBooks
twitter@SerenBooks

The right of Vanessa Lampert to be identified as
the author of this work has been asserted in accordance
with the Copyright, Designs and Patents Act, 1988.

ISBN: 978-1-78172-701-0
Ebook: 978-1-78172-704-1

A CIP record for this title is available from the British Library.

The publisher acknowledges the financial assistance of the Books Council of Wales.

Cover artwork: John Brennan: 'In Your Room', 2022, oil on canvas. Artist's
collection.

Printed in Bembo by Severn, Gloucester

Contents

Not Like This Park

My park will be a bowl to hold sunlight,
the sky dropped on long loan.
Shade no one would need to call *the shadows*.
No crouching spikes of glass in grass
by rusty swings, no busted drinking fountain
left for years, no *Fuck off* gouged on a bench
by an angry hand, no harm, no drinking,
no bargaining, nor pleading with God for out.
My park will be the out, with a café painted yellow,
where we'll watch a woman in an apron
fill a cake with raspberries and whipped cream.
No dogs bred for menace, routinely whipped,
their owners beaten or broken.
No men staring at Betfair on iPhones,
no polystyrene takeaway trays, no greasy paper
blowing over the grass like fallen cloud.
No bags of shit dangling from branches
like baubles, no man hanging, no police car,
no plastic police tape pulled taut.
No note in a freezer bag tied to a tree, saying
babe oh why, the boys? No flowers left there
cheap and dying, and drying or already dead.
My park will have great beds of roses, white
roses, their stems unbroken, no one to break them,
no one in my park but us. The warm weight
of your hand in my hand. High up there
fistfuls of stars, all hidden, and us
not needing to wait until dark
to know they'll keep coming back.

Limpet

I tried so hard to wrench you off a rock
and who could blame me? I was
only a barefoot child, hell-bent

on control. All I really wanted
was to see beneath your roof,
small apology-for-nothing

little muscle-in-a-hill. Stubborn
boarded-up-building
made for a life that wouldn't budge.

And what of all my surreptitious
wrenching? I think I was
ashamed to want to plunder

your dark cabin, quiet companion
of the ocean, quite content
to be alone. I was seen

and pulled up short as children are,
collected up your dishes
and took them home.

Little caramel-inside-a-shell,
sealed cubicle of wet.
Salty living thing that told me *No.*

Sand

On Woolacombe beach my Grandpa builds
an MG convertible sports car from sand
in front of the swingboats where I was sick once.

My car faces the wind-ruffled sea, roof down
under a sky made of torn strips of paper.
Grandpa slowly carves the bonnet and makes me

a member of the AA. He shapes the wheels
and stands back, proud as a car salesman.
Other kids are staring. They want to be me.

In a few weeks my parents will separate,
but now our orange windbreak holds them
close together in flowery beach chairs,

safe from the wind. I sit behind the steering wheel
of my new MG. The engine starts first try.
I take her out for a spin to Lundy Island

to see the puffins and the granite stacks
and back, beeping my horn to warn the surfers,
who wave. I park her where she was before,

facing out to sea. Mum looks up from her book
and says *it must be time for a 99.*
I want to jump on my car before we leave,

and ruin her so no one else can ruin her,
but Grandpa won't let me. He takes my hand
in his, saying *don't look back. Let's go.*

Tower

My father took me to London
when my whole fist could fit
inside his palm.

On the tube he lifted me up
and, holding tight, stepped out
from our carriage to the next
through the filthy hurtling dark
to thrill me, then did it again.

By the river he bought chestnuts
roasted on a brazier.

My red gloves swung on strings.
I looked up at the tower of him,
and grief would never dare
to touch my life.

Stopper

The sun is winched high in the sky
above the young men in their long shorts
who hurtle across the sand dunes,

down the beach and into the sea
carrying dirty noise in their mouths
and an inflatable woman over their heads.

They're drunk or high in the heatwave,
free falling through the promised land
that lies between boy and man.

They know everything there is to know
about how to love a woman.
Not a single one is thinking about

how long life might be this good, this sweet.
Children are watching open-mouthed,
sand on all their knees and hands like glitter,

in swimsuits with sharks and flowers
while the young men take turns
to mount the inflatable woman

lying plump and silent on an ocean-sized
bed of salt water with her red mouth
open, and her smooth pink legs

open, and her eyes fixed on the sky.
She waits for the real woman who'll lift
her yellow skirt and wade into the water

all the way to her freckled thighs
to make those young men boys again,
by shouting *pack that in and grow up.*

Then one will pull out the stopper
from the inflatable woman's shoulder
and another will hold her around the waist

and squeeze all the breath from her body.
And the boy who's closest to being a man
will hold up his hands and say *sorry. Sorry.*

Mark My Words

By Shotover Hill, where dogs run
forever over the wind-whipped green,

is the derelict pub where I worked
on Sundays. A drinkers' pub

where men stood in a line at the bar
shoulder to shoulder on yellow lino,

leaning in to their pints of Harp Extra,
eking out the weekend, pushing in hard

to the brink of Monday. Men
who thumbed coins into a juke box

so they could hear Real Men's music.
Rock bands with savage guitars,

drums that punched you in the face.
Men with names like Fat Mark,

and Todger and Corgi Registered Ian.
Men who took lip from no one. Men

who gave as good as they got. Men
who slid their empty glasses across the bar

saying *put another one in there pet,*
and sometimes, *have one yourself.*

Men who reached into the pockets
of their weekend jeans for the change,

with a working man's hand
that was never clean. Men who came

to get drunk for the feeling of being
broken open. Men who knew

Monday was coming. Men
like the one who said, *you mark my words*

when you've finished college
you won't be seen dead in a place like this.

His Cars

Looking like James Dean, my future Dad
leans on the bonnet of his first car,
a black 1950s Riley RME. He's joined at the hip
to a woman in a pink headscarf,
who only has eyes for him. In a couple of years
when that car finally gives up the ghost,
he'll push it into a ditch and walk home,
replace it with a pale blue Hillman Minx,
same woman in the passenger seat.
A toddler and a baby asleep in a carrycot
are loose in the back. The toddler
will bury the car keys in the sand at Carbis Bay
and my Dad will drive us home to St Albans
with a Kirby grip in the ignition.
There's a sludge-coloured Renault for a while,
and for donkey's years a bottle green Citroën
and before that, between marriages,
a scarlet Alfa Romeo briefly owned, loved,
unsuitable for a second family.
My Dad at the wheel with a lit cigarette,
fetching and carrying us straight from work
through rush hour from Mum's house
to his house and back, alternate weekends, year in
year out. He never missed a single chance
to see us. I'd like to take my Dad for a drive
somewhere in my white Fiat 500. I'd like to say,
'Where shall we go, Dad? Anywhere you like.'

In The Olden Days

No word of a lie, contraception wasn't a thing like it is now. The kids just kept coming if they wanted to and if they didn't, you put it down to God's mood. You didn't have a clue how far gone you were, or what you were having. There were no scans or anything. You had to just wait and see what turned up on the day, then get someone to ring round with the news and be quick about it because of the phone bill. I was lucky to have a girl after so many boys, I know that. We had this chap lay our stair carpet who said he had 8 boys. Imagine that if you will. He actually asked me how we got a girl. I told him it wasn't anything different. As far as I remember, it was just the same as usual, Saturday night after The Two Ronnies.

Letter

When the baby comes, we let the allotment
go to rack and ruin. Nettles, thistles
choke the earth's throat, and the baby rallies
each morning into life. The letter says
PLEASE keep control or surrender your plot.
We dig with the baby swaddled asleep
or screaming, and sow all our crops
in tender broken rows. That summer
the sound of water from a hose
makes the baby laugh to make light
of a stifling afternoon. Then they come,
the other gardeners, one by one, to touch
his tiny hand, his head. It's what we do
on our best days, lay down our tools, forgive.

Belonging

Same walk home under the same clean sky,
almost the weekend. Man with a parrot
on the green. Old tattoos climb his forearms,
vigorous as *Clematis Montana*.
His parrot flies in a deluge of blue over grass.
You're dying to ask, why a bird, why a parrot,
can it really love you better than a pug?
The bird lands hard on his shoulder, a gesture
that insists *you're mine*. It eyes you
dressed in its suit of pristine colour, felt tips,
Christmas baubles, the sun's face
pressed against stained glass. You're transfixed.
The bird produces fluff from the gold envelope
of its breast. *She's itchy* the man says.
She pecks at his ear and takes off. East she glides
in a casual arc, cuts the corner, then north
near the earth and far from fruit, from family
and foliage, wings outstretched like Christ's arms.
Loose and steady she turns to the west,
offering her faith to the breeze.
The man sighs, *two grand she cost me,*
worth every penny. Onwards she soars,
south by the pub, skirting a boy on a scooter.
You say *why does your parrot come back,*
when she could be free? The man shrugs,
She's a blue crested Macaw. Search me.

Oh Jossers We

Here come the circus folk, self-assured, lithe,
justifying summer with their thighs.
They're lighting up the village green like blossom.
Retro-chic and velvety, juggling old cutlery,
qualmless and oblivious to cold.
See them expertly erecting their marquees,
pirouetting, irresistible to doves.
I almost ran away to join them way back when.
I had core strength and was not shunned
by ponies. Oh jossers we, who have not clung
to the trapeze, nor held aloft a woman
on one hand. We who failed to sail through air
whilst smiling fiercely, now merely witness
all this fearless allure. See them safe
inside their neon painted spandex,
shining like a shoal of jubilant fish.
If this is a dream then hide the truth
from me. There are so many lovely things
that we can't hold or keep. I won't be a girl again
nor ever you a boy. Still they come to mingle
amongst us, bohemian and tumbling,
hula-hooping, reaping what they sow. Oh come again,
restore us. Hang by your teeth and spin for us,
for we have loved you longer than our lives.

Josser: circus word for an outsider

Sheffield

When you go to Sheffield to stay with your friend, she will meet you at the station with a piece of falafel squashed on her sweatshirt, above the place her breast was until last May. When you point out the falafel she will laugh, pick it off and eat it. To reach her back garden you will go under an archway between houses and walk along a path running through other people's gardens. You will follow her, closing each low gate behind you. On the way your friend will offer to hold a neighbour's baby while she hangs out her washing. Your friend will sway and sing *Mr Brightside* to the baby, a boy dressed in mustard-coloured dungarees. Your friend's birthday will fall on a summer Sunday. She will pull a box of vegetarian sausage rolls from a heavily iced-up freezer in the early afternoon and cook them for her party in a greasy gas oven. Between four and five, people will come to the back door with food and birthday cards. They will kiss each other then sit on cushions in a garden with a walnut tree and a privy with a broken door at the far end. Its lavatory pan will contain a pool of dark green algae-coloured water. You will try the flush and find it broken. One of the guests will arrive late with half a cantaloupe melon she's carried through the warm streets balanced on the palm of her hand. She'll say that she planned to bring the whole melon but last night it just looked so nice.

Donor

I guess your body must have always had
those extra special cells, tucked inside your bones,
long before their place in someone else's story

was announced. Once those cells belonged
to you and you alone. Watching your team smash it
two–nil at home, roasting a chicken with lemon,

walking the dog in the early morning, when the sky
above the park turns pink and it's just for you.
You weren't to know someone in a lab coat

in a lab was doing the maths, narrowing the odds,
solving a problem that wasn't yours. Preparing to give
your cells a starring role, where they would appear

as the answer. You weren't to know
that a woman was waiting for your cells to be offered
to her body so they could bloom like a dahlia

in November, flaring orange against the frost,
when summer had seemed lost forever. Now you must live
with the gratitude. And didn't you say

what you most feared was a marching band
and shiny helium balloons saying THANK YOU?
Cheerleaders with red pompoms, performing routines

in the street outside your house, all of them
chanting *thank you*. Didn't you say that kind
of thank you would make you want to ask

for your stem cells back? Isn't your kind of thank you
a handshake, a beer, and the words *cheers mate*?
Like the one that's modelled by the husband

of the woman who's alive because you gave
your stem cells to her. And now it's her turn.
She calls you her brother, in a shy way, and you call her

your sister, because you never had a sister
until now. Sister. Her good cells, your
good cells. Brother. Your sweet life, and hers.

Toads

I liked it when the road outside our old house
was dotted with toads, their eyes more golden
than you'd think, their bodies dry and low,

the colours of old leaves. I asked a woman
wearing serious shoes *what's happening?*
She said the toads walked home to spawn,

they did it every spring, brought the street to life.
Toads all roaring the same *love-me-love-me-*
fuck-me call that sounded like a marble rolling

over hard ridged plastic. I liked that the street
was full of people in green tabards marked
TOAD PATROL, saving the toads from cars,

bending and lifting every living toad,
singing as they ferried those toads from danger,
casually dismantling peril in matching clothes.

My favourites were the ones that sang
You're gonna be alright. I liked that I had a woman
to question, because I had so many. I was a girl

out on the street with my baby in a purple sling,
crying. I was just trying to soothe him with all I had
which, after milk, after clean and dry was to sing.

Did he cry less beneath open sky? Maybe
I imagined it because I wasn't alone out there,
toads and kindness and the weather finally

turning warm. I liked how people stopped traffic
by raising an arm, looking certain, looking stern.
I liked that fast men in fast cars were inconvenienced

by toads, slowly making their way in straight lines
to the place where all the sex was happening.
I liked that some people were late because others knew

toads were soft, and matterful. I liked that
after spawning, every one of those toads was free
from family ties. I told none of this to the baby.

Easy Does It

Miles of fields, a few cities. Blaze and beginning
is what we bolstered between us
and the old life, fled it early as daybreak,

easy as *never look back*. In our new street
you misjudged and clipped the wing-mirror
clean off a neighbour's Nova, our faces

looking up at us, fractured on the tarmac.
Mid-hill we found our new house by the chip shop,
its walled garden, fruit trees, and old flagstones

where silver-wet snails wrote their slow procedures.
Achy breaky heart played all summer. Our boy
marked the beat barefoot in his bouncer.

We were twenty minutes from the restless sea
where infinity waited for us,
dependable as the wind's whip on sand.

Homewards, salty, we stopped for supplies.
I was breathless, swollen, nine months gone.
You lifted our boy onto your shoulders and ran.

I raced you down the aisles. Someone said
easy does it. We were untethered,
headlong. We would always be this young.

The Size of It

Days after his birth, dazed with love,
I leave the house, my baby son
warm beneath my jacket.

He's wearing the red hat
that took one evening to knit. It's too big,
that's how small his head is.

He's so young, as yet he has no name,
and I step into the path of a cyclist
careering down the hill

who clips my side, not hard enough
to hurt me, but hurtles into
an awful cartwheel across the road.

He stands to drag his buckled
bike my way, to name for me
the thing that might have happened.

His finger points, his mouth
prepares to shout.
Then, catching sight

of the tiny child, he lifts
the palms of his wounded hands,
and silently turns to go.

It's taken half my life to learn
another mother loved that man
whose name I'll never know.

Elegy for Two Placentas

You were the image of one another.
Made of me, by me, two years apart,
entirely unearned. Made not for me,
in this body's hidden wet. No thought of mine
was needed, nor gesture of praise did I offer
the two of you, that came through me
into the dry lit world. Made to be lost
when your work was done. Cast into light,
when I was blind to the miracle that circled
back to give of itself once more
and found me yet still blind. Forgive me
for how it was, when the world was only baby
and baby again. My only boy, my girl,
the sky and every star. I swear, even the sun
seemed mine when you were all and softly done.
I was lost to him, and after lost to her.
How unassuming you were.
Slipped into the room after they had come.
Modest finale, no commentary nor ceremony,
I should have said thank you
though you could not have pleased me then.
Oh unlovely fate of the unlovely. Oh strange trees
of purple flesh and red. Oh trees
that bore a single human fruit.
I know someone held you, someone else
the other of you two years on.
I know they found you both complete and spent.
I had no questions. My body merely gave me
what I wished for. I didn't want to eat you
or bury you beneath a moon laden with light.
I wanted to forget you, humble female servants.
Loyal other mothers that came from the dark.

Birthday Magic

On my birthday, Mel takes me back to her childhood.
She knows me, knows I want to play the game
where you pull the end of a pink balloon
over the tap, fill it with hot water, tie a knot
and there you have it, a baby, warm and fragile.
We tuck the babies up our T-shirts
and give birth squatting, then wrap them in blankets
to walk round her garden, cradling them
and singing lullabies. I'm so happy being a mummy
I could burst, but instead I move the baby around.
Sometimes, when she's windy I hold her
against my shoulder, other times I lay her
on a blanket on the lawn and she looks up at the sky
kicking her little legs with me watching over.
Sometimes she's grouchy and won't be put down.
Now and again, I arrange to meet up with Mel
and we talk about our babies and jiggle them.
I say *she's had me up all night the little tinker*
and Mel says *tell me about it, this one's
got a tooth coming through, nightmare* and then
one of our babies starts crying and that's the end
of our conversation until tea, by which time
we've been walking up and down all day,
our arms aching, our babies not wanting
to be put down. Then Mel looks at me and says
let's do it! and we throw our babies as hard as we can
against the wall and watch them explode.
We laugh at the sound of it, at the two whopping
wet stains on the brick and the small scraps
of pink rubber lying on the patio,
and when we grow up, she doesn't have
her three children and I don't have my two.
We have that other life, the one without them.

Woodland

At the poetry festival, the gorgeous boy poets
are taking turns to read poems about kneeling
in woodland or being knelt before by boys who may

or may not be poets. The girl poets are listening
as girl poets do. Some are aching from sitting
for hours, hearing about the boy poets coming

in woodland without them. Some are thinking
of the winter woodland months, of the cold
or wet, or both and the fact that it might be

totally fucking worth it. Others are thinking
glad thoughts about how lucky they are to be girls
with skirts you can theoretically lift in woodland,

without wet trousers it could be a win win
wet woodland wise. One girl poet has pale legs.
She thinks about the price of tights, their fragile weave

on the wet woodland floor. She'd like to read
poems about men kneeling for women in woodland
or women kneeling for women in woodland.

She'd like to read poems about women kneeling
for men on a rug in woodland during a warm spell.
She has not read every poem about woodland, if there are

any poems that address the above, then Respect.
She's just saying, she'd like to read of a clitoris
in woodland. She's just saying *vulva,* twice. *Vulva.*

Those Who Remember World War II

In dwindling numbers, they still
keep shtum about the war, do their best

to put it behind them. Let my mum,
Vionne, be counted as one. As yet

unborn when it began, she was named
after a village in France, where someone

long gone now was stationed or
maybe they were just passing through.

I don't know. Nothing remains
of the story except my mum who,

having lived through all those years
of rationing, can't abide bananas.

On Mother's Day

He invites his mother for lunch. The house hums with quiet hope. It's in the food he's bought, and in the words of songs on the radio. He polishes the windows until his arm throbs. Expectation sparks at the tip of the match. He lights the candle and its flame carries the scent of oranges. He takes the rugs into the garden and shakes them. Hope is there too, tired old thing refreshed. He hasn't seen his mother since she died when he was eleven. Her absence has hovered low over his life. But as he watches her walk slowly up the path, he feels spent sorrow peel away like dry skin. Later he will expect to find flakes inside his clothes, but there will be nothing. At first his mother doesn't speak but holds his grown man face in her hands. His beard is between the spread of her fingers and she looks up at him with her eyes an ancient wet blue. *My boy.* She straightens his glasses. All morning they chat with her in the chair by the window where the light falls as he moves about preparing food; meat with rich gravy, dumplings, runner beans, cabbage, roast potatoes, the kind of food they last ate together. At the table they sit opposite one another. Both eat everything set before them. Then there is treacle tart and custard. Afterwards he drives to the river and they walk along the towpath where primroses stagger yellow up the bank. She says *look at them in their spring frocks* and points, her arm inside her dark green wool coat. There are rowers on the water and they watch them for a while, before he takes her arm and they walk back to the bridge where the car is parked. At home he makes tea and they agree that she should leave quietly like last time. But this time he will know it is going to happen. He tells her that the sign will be when he goes to the sink to wash the cups. He rinses for a long time with the tap running. Though he is listening for it, he doesn't hear the click of the front door. As he turns to walk to the window, he sees the day step back from him with his mother inside it.

Duty

Before the girl from 4Y, let's call her Lisa,
became Locust Monitor, that job was mine.

A sense of duty came easily to me.
I picked them the greenest youngest privet,

refreshed their water, paid them a cheerful
daily visit, pulled younger kids into the lab

when the hoppers hatched, so they could be
repelled. Maybe I was born for this,

to tend to the needs of others. I clean
my mother's pond filter without complaint.

I unclog, degrease. I stood on the touchline
all those Sundays in sleet. When the locusts bred

with rampant ease, yours truly prepared
the ether and prayed for their souls.

Lisa, they weren't asking for much.
No locust ate another on my watch.

Likes You

The girl who used to bully you at school calls
and leaves a voicemail, asking for acupuncture.

She wants you to go to her house,
that's how bad the pain is, and there's a family

on holiday in France and it's your family
forty years ago. You're a little girl

eating a croissant for the first time and the ants
are huge and all the dogs might have rabies

don't approach them. It's sunny every day
and your mum plays frisbee with you in the sea

but the best part of all is the 14 whole days
of not being hurt by the girl at school

who makes hurting you her project.
And someone is washing blood from a pavement

and it's her blood because for years, you made
all the spilt blood her blood. And now

she lives in a house with a yellow front door
in a street named after a small songbird

and you're in her bedroom, sitting on her bed,
both pretending you've never met before.

She's lying face down, with all the needles in
and suddenly, what you want to say is

*the thing that made you bully me, can you still
see that in me now?* And what you want to happen

is the miracle where you take the needles out
and she stands up pain free, and likes you.

Happy Family Soliloquy

Conflict? I survive it, I'm hell-bent
on healing every rift. Love's certainty
will always wait for me. People.
More than the world, they want to live in me,
seek a swift departure from the shambles
of before. It's not their fault. I lead
by example, hold my hands up,
on occasion, I'm absent. If only
I could be there for them all.
I'm a triumph of show over tell,
a machine of solace. I raise the us
above solus. Admittedly, kinship
was once a necessity. Now?
Not necessarily. I'll prop my door ajar
for their fickle shifts in fashion.
I'm a sweet kingdom of complexity.
See me duck and weave for every whim.
I only exist to hold them, console them.
They can't be blamed for wanting
more than the world to live in me.
I'm a fortress of trust and stories.
Their table could be my table. Their garden,
its peonies and patio, each fruit tree mine.
Mine every one of their children.
Little wonder that more than the world
they want to live in me. They ache
to assemble the rumour. Warm haven
me, ancient circle. From here
heaven is nearer than they'll know.

Some Pleasures

Platinum, for its hardness, how it doesn't tarnish.
Poodles that lie on their backs
on your lap, front paws folded down.

The cold precision of scissors, pinking shears
for their name. A Steradent tablet dropped
into a glass of water, for the plop and the long

fizz of air leaving. Removing a man's tie,
the word *gravel*. Platinum was once tossed aside,
worthless, overshadowed by gold.

Chipping old tiles off a wall, but only
when they come away easily, agreeing enough
is enough. The Radiohead song that begins

a green plastic watering can. The sound barn owls make
when they mate. Pushing a thumb through the skin
of a satsuma in the run-up to Christmas. Bookmarks,

binoculars, cherry ice cream. Daydreaming
about next time round being a childless silversmith.
Couscous. Lisbon existing over the sea

without me. Opening the window of a train
as it speeds through open countryside, taking off
my platinum wedding ring. Throwing it.

Say it, Hiker

It's too easy to let lonely win the fight.
The kids are with their dad alternate weekends.
It kicks like a horse but don't you get to hike?
Look at you, wind-tousled in your turquoise
gore-tex cagoule and gaiters. Say it, hiker.
There's always something lying around
to lift us. The box of eggs slipped
from your hand. Four broke, but two didn't
and the meringue was good. Ripe strawberries
at Aldi, double cream on special. Raise your spoon
you're a hiker, you'll burn it off uphill.
Think of all those Fridays you're footloose
to drive to the Lake District after work,
handbrake on in time for last orders.
Think of that guy in the pub who said
seven hours on the road, you must be hard-core
or mental, offered you a crisp, not a drink,
meaning he didn't fancy you, leaving you free
to act normal. Think of how, when it turned out
he did fancy you, near the summit of Lonscale Fell,
it was a cinch to remember that drink
and hike harder. Think of the view you won
when you were champion of the unspoiled wet world.
Wasn't the walk back down easy?
Each footfall a countdown to sea level,
where the tide toys with shells and worn glass.
Gratitude waits to lead you by the hand,
points out all the blues and greens,
the crystals of dry salt. The constant tide
turning. Keeping its hold on the light.

Call

My girl's a woman now and I've lost time
distracted. She's earbud plugged into hip-hop,

I wouldn't really know where to shop
to buy the stuff she'd hug me for.

The pub's shut, austerity bearing down,
but there are kids slick with factor 50,

chasing each other in the heat, who know
this is all there is that ever mattered.

They're queuing for ice creams at the pool,
but my girl's upstream by the river

with her friends. Somewhere near the weir,
where I once saw a small brown dog

trembling, too frightened to cross the bridge
above the terrible churn and roar.

And I'm cycling to work thinking
there's nothing in this world I wouldn't give

for her to be small again, just for half a day –
all the tenderness back, reaching out her arms,

toes curled over the pool's long drop,
and my call, *Jump, Jump. You can do it all.*

The Crux

Through layers of Christmas
you come back to haunt us,

the sink's greasy burden
unmanned by your absence,

the turkey more lunged at
than carved. How many years

since you ended it, eleven?
My mind's eye has you restless

as you were. Muscular and lean
as a much younger man

thanks to all that running,
which, as it turned out

was away. You left us to guess
what hell it was

that hunted you. That's the crux
of what's haunting us now.

Running

I'm running through a scenario
in which my brother John, is alive after all.

John eating sausages with mustard. John
running someone to the station. John

not letting age stand between him
and the lycra he likes to run in. Look at John,

giving a younger man a run for his money.
John's a whippet, admit it, he's fast

for a man of his age. Slim too. John hasn't
run to fat. True, when he runs a comb through,

John's aware his hair's thin. Who cares.
That's run of the mill, that's to be expected.

Yes. John's got his life running smoothly.
Whatever he does, John's alive.

He's running a five-a-side tournament. All four
of his boys are in it. John pours cold drinks.

Later he'll run the little one a bath.
At weekends John runs on the embankment

with his dog. John has the whole sky,
John won't die, he's run through everything.

Most of it wasn't his fault.
John's just running, nothing to run from.

When You Are King

More than the need for a sign
from an absent God, more than
a clear view of Venus from a Cornish cliff,

more than seeking a cure for grief
or not speaking your name
for fear anger will spoil the day, I say

it's time to make you king of something,
because surely even the dead
should be kings, their subjects crying

there's nothing to forgive.
I saved the football card you found
in a box of cereal. You stood on your chair

to show us your hero Gordon Banks
shouting *it's my lucky day,* because you loved
that man with a small boy's clean love –

which hovered and burned with certainty
that your life would turn out something like the life
of a famous England goalkeeper.

Only the living can crown the dead,
so I'm making your life like Gordon's.
I'm making you squint under a bright sun

framed in a sky of roaring blue,
with a tan like Gordon's, in a yellow shirt
like Gordon's, three lions on your chest.

You're holding the ball you've saved
and you'll save again. You have to be brave
to be goalie because the whole team pays

for your mistakes. I've hidden your photo
in a box of cereal. A small boy will find you.
He'll say *this man is a king,* and he'll save you.

Wimbledon 2020

I'm changing what happened.
In the new truth, my dad did not die young.
He's out on the street in front of his house
with his old man's face lifted
to a cloudless sky, brilliant summer.
A purple hot air balloon floats
high over the city he chose
for its famous bridge, and a woman
who loved him for a while.
He's standing to watch the balloon drift,
waiting for the roar and the orange blast of fire.
He says science and magic don't fall out,
they just stay with what they know.
Years ago, he fixed a hole in his garage roof.
All afternoon, a blackbird flitted and sang
a song that pleaded for mercy.
She had built her nest in a dry building
with a skylight that was now a prison
with her chicks inside.
So my dad climbed back up his ladder
with a hammer and opened, for that bird,
a brand new door to her sky. Now he walks
slowly to Clifton Village for ice cream.
Really good, bad ice cream with cookie dough
and caramel sauce pooled in the middle.
And I'm on my way, driving south
on the road that leads to him.
We'll watch the tennis and whichever man wins
my dad will cry, then go outside
and cut the grass. I'll stand at the window
to see him smile to himself, because he saw
the dreams of another man come true,
and he saw that man kiss a shining trophy
then raise it to show the sky.
My dad will put the lawnmower away
in a garage with a leaky roof

and come back in. He'll give me a spoon
to go first and we'll eat ice cream
straight from the tub, because my dad
knows how to take a victory and make it
his victory, and my victory.

Margate in September

If there's sand and you can let yourself,
what is there to do on a beach but dig?
We dig, the boy and me with our hands
and the old red spade because it's back to school
tomorrow and back to work tomorrow,
and today the sun still thinks it's June,
spreading loose glory over the sea, over us
with our gorgeous and our ungorgeous bare skin,
and we're pushing ourselves right up to the margin
of the last page of summer, digging an island
as the tide comes in, salt water reaching
to take back what we borrow, and it must be
the boy's thrill that calls the others. Kids,
and tattooed men with shovels. A tribe of diggers,
that's what we are, with a drum'n'bass soundtrack
rising from somewhere, and us digging to the beat,
digging ourselves an island until it's a thing
of greatness with us on top, water all around
in the almost evening, holding our spades,
our ice creams and beer. Everyone together,
not digging now, but thinking our separate thoughts
of all that's scared and incomplete,
here's the marvellous thing we finished.

What the Horses Told Us

This is how you wait for me, silent
in the churchyard with stones of the forgotten
or remembered in flowers, the heart's need to gild.

In your pram you liked the shade. Now
from beneath your tree, you scan the green
of a valley's wet morning. Sometimes

I watch you walk towards me. When I can't
it's because the loneliness is there,
making the shape of you again, its friend.

It's a dead weight I have neither map nor might
to bear. I'm pretty sure I've never had God
but if he were here, I'd give him to you.

I'll keep today, you smiling at our stories.
How the morning braided us together
and autumn rhymed her stride with ours

and showed us the places she worked,
with her red-threaded needle, laughing
at the apples we stooped to gather.

The horses took them from us, bit down to taste
the juice of what was saved. They knew
that nothing greater touched this earth.

Snow

Just as I start becoming a more decent person
a past unkindness will fall, silent as snow
from the dark, to settle cold on me

like the pink hopscotch grid I recognise
because I chalked it outside the bungalow
of the two little girls, same day they moved in.

We wanted to play but they shook their heads
no, just stood there in matching red dresses
watching us in silence, holding hands

as we made that game seem more fun
than it was, giggling, leaping,
catching each other's eye as if we sisters

loved one other way more than we did.
We never thought to give them
a second chance. By the end of winter

they'd gone because their bungalow
burned down in the snow. The whole street
turned out to see two little girls

silently holding hands, snow
on their shoulders, snow in their hair
while the windows glowed fierce orange

and cracked. No one cried, no one spoke,
and dirty smoke parted the falling snow
like it knew where it was going.

Homing Pigeons

Here's the 70's, lime green, geometric.
Coleslaw is the old hummus.

Here's the stepfather, night-worker, hard man,
who surrenders all his daylight hours to sleep.

Here's the place of *watch your step*
where fear and worry limber up

to rise with the man when he wakes.
Here, for the children fiercely shushed,

his kindnesses are unexpected blessings.
Here's the morning he gives them a box,

here their shy approach, their hope
for a sign, the smallest rustle, just a coo

to believe him when he says it holds
two birds. Inside the pigeons wait

with folded wings, all the longing ache
of darkness for its end. Sometimes freedom

is the sky returned by children.
Now the churning rise of release,

now the desperate feathered race.
Never look back. Get out of this place.

Boys

Last June my sister released
a young cockerel in the university arboretum
when it revealed its gender by crowing

experimentally in a hoarse voice.
Her partner used to wring the cocks' necks
while listening to hip-hop but then he left.

Now I'm at the garage filling up with petrol,
and pinned to the counter is a mugshot
of a cockerel, blown-up A4.

Its prehistoric face peers out, red wattles,
a comb styled to the left like Elvis
and a cravat of fine gold satin feathers.

Underneath it says *is this your cock?*
I take a picture, WhatsApp my sister,
your bird? Second chance?

She replies *no fucking way,*
promiscuous creatures that upset
the neighbours, and tear

members of their own family
to pieces. I've enough of that
on my plate with the boys.

Mount Toubkal

I'm walking up this mountain for the sky
and because my decree absolute arrived,
so I need to see something through

to an end all parties agree on.
No living thing can thrive here. The air
is thin, weighty with dust. Near the top

a woman called Sue says she maintains
all the stiles in Oxfordshire and Gloucestershire,
and a man called Ian says he trades

in Fibonacci ratios. He says his job
is a real conversation stopper with women.
In the thrumming silence I imagine

Sue in walking boots striding over a wet green
landscape wearing a sturdy rucksack
that holds a hammer, nails, and a cheese roll.

It's getting hard to breathe. Ian starts to cry
and a guide escorts him down the mountain.
At the summit we enter a flimsy cloud

that shifts to offer glimpses of graffiti
and litter. My heart thumps in my ears.
Were Ian here, I'd ask what his job entails.

Cornish Morning

Now blooming pink puffs of thrift, and puffs
of lilac scabious wander over the cliff path.
Now sea campion and celandine, now sun
fires this morning ruthless bright. No sadness
has followed us here this time, no loss,
and we walk where a skylark hangs his song
above a gulley where a shipwreck rusts.
No life was lost, and the gorse sings fierce
of yellow. A flock of migrant wheatears
alights in a field by the path. Now the pale
aquamarine sea, now black lichen and green
grow on granite. Now warbler and chough
trust their wings to the roughshod wind. It's enough.
Today there's nothing left for us to mourn.

Flight

If he were a bird there'd be feathers.
Long plumes in the bedroom, downy fluff
in the salad crisper. He'd be majestic

in his plumage, proud, unflappable.
The two of you are up there now,
fledglings, each one for the other.

Gentle over the fragile bones,
unearthing the buried sorrows,
turning them in your slow, young hands.

I'm thinking of the sprinting heart,
its singularity, of you learning
all there is to know of the nest.

Where we came from, where we go,
wind in all our feathers, ruffling change
and there's this thing I'm keeping.

There was a time before wings,
before the knowledge
of flight, when you were only mine.

Budgie

I'm getting my own budgie in yellow,
a girl one with her own toys. A swinging perch,
a pink mirror and a bell on a chain to ring

whenever the fancy takes her. Budgies want
stimulation. I'll keep her in a deluxe cage,
bespoke, my height five-two, so we can talk

eye to eye. You have to win their trust
early doors. I'll keep everything wiped down
spotless and she'll have her own wall to wall

carpet made from my Top Santé magazine
changed regular as clockwork. I'll wedge
a cuttlefish between the bars, and open

her little door Saturday nights. She'll be free
to soar through the maisonette no holds barred.
She'll probably settle on my shoulder

while *Strictly*'s on but maybe she won't.
That's her business. I'm getting a blanket
to throw over her cage. She's going to need me

to choose when's night and day for her.
That will be down to what I'm feeling
on the day, up to me to decide when it's over.

Golden Hamster Elegy

Inquisitive vermin, pocket-sized, silent,
you came as a solution, a balm
to soothe disappointment, when we refused
to buy the children a horse, a dalmatian,

a chinchilla, a canary and a mouse.
I don't recall the final tally of you,
small creatures who didn't bite,
whose babies were the size of baked beans.

How trustingly we delivered your bodies
into the hands of children. How predictably
your cheeks bulged with seeds. How constantly
you remained sturdy vessels for love.

Chutney, Noodles, Alan, Thierry Henry
we signed your names on birthday cards
in a hamster's shaky paw, though you were not
family. You were our prisoners, caged

one after another, after another.
Your choices were those of a lifer's,
so you slept in the jam jar we offered you
to pee in, and always peed in your bed.

We saw mindfulness when you ran –
in the wheel that leads nowhere, nodded sagely
at your running commentary on life.
You held up a mirror when you fought

after mating, choosing to raise your kids alone.
When released for exercise on the kitchen floor,
you stayed close to the skirting board, wary
of birds that might swoop from a sky

you would never see. Gilded rodent,
stub-tailed friend, who through gentleness
taught us to be gentle, I wish I'd thought
to offer you a glimpse of sky.

Black and White

I went to an exhibition. Black and white
portraits of the dogs that searched

the wreckage of the twin towers,
or were there to bring solace to the living.

Giving whatever they had. I don't know
what they had. Someone decided,

after this, the work of those dogs
was done. I watched as one by one,

a line of people leaned in, to be
as close to those dogs as they could.

Some read their stories out loud
in that gallery built high over the sea,

with great windows that frame the sky,
as if to try and hold it steady for a while.

Those dogs looked pretty ordinary to me.
One had grey eyebrows and a bone.

Another lay asleep beneath a blanket
of sunlight. I don't know what a dog

remembers, or feels, or forgets.
I don't know if it was right or wrong

to retire them. If it was wrong,
please God make me wrong like that.

Dig Deeper

Brunch, fuck it, misdemeanour,
I'll have the artichoke, are a few words

not said by my mum. It's *rabbits*
rabbits rabbits down the phone at six

on May Day morning, and, *that ruddy heron*
has eaten all my fish. I wish we could move

overseas where they don't have limescale.
Do you know how much I love cheese?

A long time ago she told me, *hate*
is a very strong word, dig deeper now.

And don't we always long to hear
I'm proud of you, keep doing what you're doing,

and isn't what she gave to me
go up, I'll mind the baby while you sleep.

When I was a child and crying,
she made me laugh by saying *no don't stop,*

you must try your best to cry harder.
Then she caught my tear in a teaspoon.

We planted it in a pot of earth.
I swear to you now, it grew.

Bedlington Terriers

Today's a wet epic of cloud, so I'm reading
about the artist Craigie Aitchison
in a book I was given last Easter. He said

the crucifixion was the most horrific
story ever told, and painted it repeatedly.
Here is a painting of an orange field,

bellowing at a wall of unwavering magenta,
where sky ought to be
and a handful of weak stars bloom.

In this one, two canaries flit across a plum
horizon; and in every painting
Christ is always pinned to the cross, dying.

Here are the paintings with Aitchison's dogs
gazing at the suffering Christ. They suffer so
He doesn't die alone. Bedlington terriers

like my sister's dog, Olive, who was lost
in a tunnel last spring. My sister lay alone
all night, praying for her dog to be saved,

and was saved by a man from the council
who, finding the manhole next morning,
raised that filthy wretch into the light.

The dog was shivering, ecstatic,
black with sewage. Forgiven,
forgiving us everything.

Still Life with Story

A corner of the park was cordoned off
with Do Not Cross police tape today.

Someone's racing bike leaned against a tree.
It was so early, new light seeped in.

Only a few dogs walking their people were out
and what happened there isn't my story

to tell. I've missed so many dawns
and their choruses for the love of sleep.

Birdsong always stays hopeful in dreams.
My friend says it's OK to tell because

people take their lives in every park.
My brother rose in a darkness

far from sunrise. Everyone else was asleep.
He washed his body for a long time

then ironed his clothes. He walked
up the lane with his dog and took

his own life. The sky above him went pink
then red, then it turned towards morning.

How to Avoid Clichés

Practice makes enough. Clichés ride
on thermals like strains of the song
you've got to search for the hero inside yourself.
Learn to duck and leave. In your mind's ear
go to the hospice where your dad stayed
for respite care then curtains, not curtains,
he died. Don't say angels, every last one
of those people, peaceful, don't say
the birds sang their hearts out, lovely garden,
fragrant pink roses or he had new pyjamas
buttoned all the way like a little boy.
Say you watched a plane fly over and pretended
it was packed with the cheerfully divorced
heading somewhere wet. Say they wore gaiters
and read badly-written blockbusters,
with stabbings they won't have seen coming.
Say there was a doctor in a green jumper
so thin you could see her bra and she was crouching
beside your dad's bed. Say she was pregnant
but you couldn't tell until she stood up,
which happened after she had recited a list
of possible happinesses for your dad
in a soft voice, whilst slowly stroking his forearm.
Say his pyjama sleeve was rolled up
past the elbow and the palm of his hand
was upturned, reminding you of a clean ashtray
or Christ. Say she stroked up his arm asking
would you like to play Scrabble? then down,
or do the sudoku together? Fancy a baguette
with ham, and a sliced tomato?
Wagner's Ring cycle on headphones?
Or maybe you'd like a whisky with ice? Don't say
if your own children turn out half as kind
as the people who work in hospices,
yours will have been a life well-lived, job done
or that you miss your dad more than ever
all these years on. Say he chose a whisky
and some pork scratchings. Say the pregnant doctor
poured him a treble. Don't call the ice rocks.

Bomb

Someone found a hand grenade
beside the River Thames,
it got a mention in the *Herald*
and then the *Oxford Times*.

Right next to the bridge there
where I take the boy to swim.
It was killingly hot last summer,
sweet relief to just wade in.

Before it was identified,
it must have been lying in wait.
Tightly bound small package
of remembered wartime fate.

Little nut of anger,
possibly coiled to spring
who knows, I couldn't tell you.
We only go there for a swim.

I don't care for the swimming pool,
its chlorine or its throng.
I prefer the peace of the river
and her unexploded bomb.

Halloween

Plastic pumpkins are stacked in Sainsbury's,
family bags of Haribos 2 for 1.
I'm driving to Mum's to see my stepfather
just discharged from ophthalmology.

He's watching the snooker in his recliner,
footrest up. Onscreen a man in a suit
leans in to pocket the pink. A plastic cup,
the size of a satsuma, is taped over

my stepfather's eye. All the colours of hurt
are under it. Violet and charcoal, mustard-
edged. His eye is puffed-up and shut.
Dark stitches and dried blood

map the contour of the socket. I say
that looks sore. He lifts the remote
to mute the volume, studies me
with his good blue eye, and a small creature

wakes in me after years of sleep.
I tell my stepfather we're going trick or treating,
with him dressed as a bluebottle. I say
all we need is a plastic cup for your good eye.

I say *let's pop you in a black bin bag
and fashion you wings from cling film
and wire coat hangers.* I say *I'll go and charge
your electric buggy in the shed.*

Then he laughs and forgiveness
is in the room, like the light from the last
candle on a birthday cake you didn't
have enough breath to blow out.

The Menopausal

Friable our minds and freighted by heat
as yet too young for chairobics,
we have consigned all g-strings to landfill,

forgetful too. What was it Elvis died of?
And if he hadn't died of what he died of,
would he be dead by now? Everything hurts,

the arches under both my feet. It's a shame
about Phil Collins. HRT will kill you.
He can barely walk, bless him. Open a window.

Canada

Nights when the moon's too heavy
I think about my ovaries – those two
low buildings stuccoed, painted pink,
those warehouses that came with me,
once teemed with tiny half-people, all cute-as,
every one clamouring to call me Mum.
Imagine those fat fists you have to kiss,
the soaring blue of their eyes. Listen,
I won't lie; many times I feared one would
storm in headlong with its big head
and list of equipment. I used to welcome
menstruation, even one time on the escalator
that exits the tube, and once in the bakery
section of Lidl. Twice I let my body
wave a baby through – how they thrived,
how they grew, see them shopping
and hanging out their wet towels.
Today a sonographer confirmed *Yep,
everything's nicely shut down in there.*
Think nailed planks over each entry
and exit, in the shape of an X.
Think windows boarded-up, graffiti
scrawled on pink. I'd like to think
the little half-people made it safely out.
I'm picturing them, looking like me
on the Isle of Wight or in Canada. Yes,
that's the place. Say it with me. Canada.

What I Learned on the Erasmus Scheme

Anthropology is easier in books.
On Lesvos Laura is 'the dirty English girl'
until she cuts her dreadlocks, then she is

'the English girl without hair' in Greek.
It sounds beautiful. *Then katalavennoh* –
I do not understand. *Eee kata stis Marias* –

the cat that belongs to Maria. *Then
katalavennoh* – I do not understand.
The Greek students make one beer last

all evening – *Alkoolikos Anglikos*.
Some words have no translation. Blue jeans –
blue jeans, pronounced *bloo tzinn*.

Attending church may aid integration.
Attending church in *bloo tzinn* will move that
further away. During menstruation

it is taboo to be seen in a swimsuit.
It's hot on the beach in tights. The Greek girls
like to go to the hot springs at Eftalou.

They float round the pool, discussing
their *pouli* – bird, a friendly word
both genders use to refer to their genitals.

They invite us to the hot springs.
We stay there all afternoon with our birds
submerged. No one mentions them.

Return

Before such time this body
fails in whichever way
or ways it surely will,

I'll need to load up the car
with all these pebbles
and return them to the beaches

I found them on, in Cornwall
mostly, and also, write down
the ways I've seen love

and been loved, like that time
on the driveway of my then-
mother-in-law's house

when our daughter told us
we had accidentally brought
Sadie the hermit crab home

from the beach, in an almost-
dry bucket and her dad, my then-
husband, reversed the car out

and drove the forty minutes
it took to get to the beach. Greg.
His name was Greg. It still is.

Student in Lesvos

Two stray dogs crisscross the streets,
skirt the shoreline, drawn like all of us
to the sea's colossal pool.

You've started looking out for them,
their tail-up trot behind strangers,
inseparable, never tiring of the search

for someone to be with. Renée says
*try harder to be a neutral observer
of island life.* So you sever

your long dreadlocks at the roots,
blades hard on skin, and it still feels
like defiance. The matted ropes fall.

Now separated you give the afternoon
a second chance, open the letter
with your name penned in purple.

Swathes of vivid flowers
circle the address, her longing
condensed to ink on paper.

On the seal a cloud of pink birds
where she put her mouth and thought
of you. Come back, it whispers.

Fly home. You let the letter fall
to your dead hair and leave the flat.
Cool sea air on your neck,

you walk to the beach, light up, inhale.
The two dogs greet you, panting,
eager for another chance to matter.

Our Song

can't be found inside a jukebox,
in a pub where people limber up with beer,
then fire up any old song to raucously

sing along, it's not that kind of song.
Our song arises in an atmosphere
of hush. It's a riverbank holiday easy sky

with a touch of high cloud drift
when we were young, lying in a field,
somewhere I forget the name of now,

your leg resting on mine. I'd like
to give our song an orchestra for free.
We'd dress up respectably, arriving

separately, and each tip our drivers
a twenty. Mine would open the door for me,
and bow because that's how damn well

I'd scrub up. We'd meet one another
in the members' bar, and raise a toast,
just the way we used to do. The soloist

would be somewhere deep backstage,
warming our song with a sherry.
She'd have sapphires and diamonds

in rows at her throat, with prisms
all brilliant with light. And when it came,
the moment she stood up to sing,

we'd be sure it was our song approaching,
by the long velvet dress she'd be wearing,
thundering scarlet in folds to the floor.

She'd introduce our song in her soft
speaking voice, like the icing you used to save
until last. Then turning to face us

she'd say *Hey you two, why not try*
giving love one more go? we're a long
time gone. And she'd sing our song.

Aldeburgh

Because the sea had no plan for us,
we took the path to the cold estuary

and found the day to be well-matched
to this island's edge mid-winter.

How small we were beneath perpetual sky.
You pointed way out over the water,

to a bundle of what looked like sticks,
and said *Is that a curlew?*

to yourself, I suppose, I wouldn't know,
but wished it to be one, the way

people who live far away from the sea
tend to, wading birds not being the kind

they could say they really knew.
And the curlew lifted her wings and flew.

End Party

More than an upgrade to anything
that goes a little faster than the last,
more than a spruced-up commitment

to kombucha, or hot yogalates,
we need biodegradable balloons,
high on helium, to let go of,

for the hell of it on a hill.
The children we once were,
are alive and well.

It's been so long since the sky
took anything I was ready
to surrender.

Let's pen new hopes on a label
and make ourselves
an occasion up there.

Nothing fancy, champagne
and a pink sunset,
no one else, only us,

watching two balloons
lean in to the whim
of the wind.

No more you my muse,
no more I your muse.
No new love

found in old love.
Just two people
standing on a hill,

letting go.

Notes on the poems

Thank you to the publishers of the following magazines and publications, in which these poems or earlier versions of them first appeared:
Poetry Wales, Quince, Tears In The Fence, The Frogmore Papers, Finished Creatures, Magma, The Moth, A Nest of Singing Birds – The Edward Cawston Thomas Prize Anthology, Ver Poets Open Competition Anthology 2020 and 2021, Fish Poetry Prize Anthology 2020, The Bedford Poetry Competition Winners Anthology 2021, Cannon Poets Sonnet or Not Poetry Competition Anthology 2021, Poetry News Autumn 2020, National Poetry Competition 2020 Winners Anthology, Verve Poetry Festival Competition Anthology 2021, Ware Poets Open Poetry Competition Anthology 2022, Live Canon International Poetry Competition 2020, 2021 and 2022, Segora Poetry Competition Anthology 2021, Ten Poems About Families – Candlestick Press 2022.

Thank you to the judges and organisations that awarded prizes to the following poems or earlier versions of them:

National Poetry Competition 2020, 'Sand' – Commended and published by The Poetry Society
Newcastle Poetry Competition 2020, 'Student in Lesvos' – Highly Commended
Café Writers Open Poetry Competition 2019, 'Canada' – 1st Prize
Edward Thomas Fellowship Poetry Competition 2020, 'Bedlington Terriers' – 1st Prize
Ver Poets Open Competition 2021, 'Say it, Hiker' (with the title 'Gratitude') – 1st Prize
Ver Poets Open Competition 2020, 'Woodland' – 1st Prize
Oxford Brookes International Poetry Competition 2020, 'How to Avoid Clichés' – 2nd Prize
Fish Poetry Prize 2020, 'Some Pleasures' – 2nd Prize
Sentinel Literary Quarterly Poetry Competition July 2021, 'Likes You' – 1st Prize
The Bedford Poetry Competition 2021, 'Halloween' – 3rd Prize
Cannon Poets Sonnet or Not Poetry Competition 2021, 'Letter' – Highly Commended
Kent and Sussex Poetry Society Open Competition 2021, 'Elegy for Two Placentas' – 2nd Prize

Troubadour International Poetry Prize 2020, 'Wimbledon 2020' – Highly Commended

The Telegraph Poetry Competition, 'Happy Family Soliloquy' – Highly Commended

The Poetry Society Members' Poems Competition Autumn 2020, Winner for 'Boys'

Café Writers Open Poetry Competition 2021, 'When You Are King' – Highly Commended

Verve Poetry Festival Competition 2021, 'Donor' – Highly Commended

Ware Poets Open Poetry Competition 2022, 'His Cars' – 2nd Prize

Live Canon International Poetry Competition 2021, 'Cornish Morning' – Shortlisted

Ver Poets Open Competition 2020, 'Dig Deeper' – Highly Commended

Segora Poetry Competition 2021, 'Flight'– Highly Commended

Ware Poets Open Poetry Competition 2022, 'Mark My Words' – Highly Commended

Live Canon International Poetry Competition 2022, 'Snow' – Longlisted

Wigtown Poetry Prize 2021, 'Homing Pigeons' – Shortlisted

Alpine Fellowship Poetry Prize 2022, 'Homing Pigeons' – Special Commendation

Gregory O'Donoghue International Poetry Competition 2019, 'What the Horses Told Us' – Commended

The following poems or earlier versions of them first appeared in my pamphlet 'On Long Loan' published by Live Canon (2020):
'Canada', 'Woodland', 'Tower', 'Margate in September', 'Not Like This Park', 'What the Horses Told Us', 'Toads', 'Oh Jossers We'.

'Birthday Magic' is for Melanie Hawkins
'Margate in September' is for George Lowman
'Black and White' is dedicated to the memory of Sandy Steele

Heartfelt thanks to my teachers at Poetry School London and Newcastle University, especially Tamar Yoseloff and Glyn Maxwell for opening the door to that MA in 2017. Glyn, it's true, the good tutorials happen in champagne bars. Thank you to my poetry tribe: Roger Bloor, Mary Mulholland, Sara Levy, Judith Wozniak, Diana Cant, Alex Corrin-Tachibana, Chrissie Dreier, Vicky Morris, and Eva O'Brien for the warmth and generosity of your friendship and for helping me become a better poet. Thank you to the members of team Sevenish, and to my family and friends for not scarpering when I poem you. Thank you to everyone at Seren for taking a chance on me, especially Rhian Edwards. Thank you to my son Adam for his unwavering patience and willingness to referee bouts of Mum v. Computer and to my daughter Sophie for her inspirational courage and spirit of joyfulness and adventure. Finally, thanks to Les McMinn for telling me I could write and making me believe it with more enduring kindness than I know how to measure.